Original title:
The Orchard's Gifts

Copyright © 2025 Creative Arts Management OÜ
All rights reserved.

Author: Jameson Hartfield
ISBN HARDBACK: 978-1-80586-407-3
ISBN PAPERBACK: 978-1-80586-879-8

**Fragrance of the Earth's Embrace**

A skunk and a squirrel, sharing a laugh,
In a garden of thyme, they calculated math.
The flowers all giggled, their petals so bright,
While bees danced to music beneath the moonlight.

The tomatoes wore hats, red and so round,
They claimed they grew wise, yet still stuck to ground.
With radishes bold in their plaid, they would boast,
Of raucous debates with the silly green ghost.

## Essence Captured in a Single Drop

In the dew of the morn, a bug finds his soap,
He scrubs all his wings, tries hard to elope.
But slippery soap sends him tumbling down,
As ladybugs giggle and watch from the crown.

A fruit fly, a dancer, spins round on his feet,
Sashaying through nectar, oh what a sweet treat!
But slipping on juice, he begins to take flight,
And crashes in laughter, what a saucy night!

## Golden Apple, Silver Moon

A golden apple swung on a proud, bending limb,
Declared itself king with a whimsical whim.
But coconuts chuckled, their shells hard as stone,
And claimed royalty's crown was just something they've grown.

The moon, rather cheeky, winked at the scene,
"Orchards are wild; have you seen what I mean?"
As stars played hopscotch with fruit flies in tow,
The laughter grew loud, oh what a great show!

## Sipping Sunlight from Dappled Skies

A silly young berry dreamed big in the sun,
Sipping sunlight, oh, what a fun run!
His seeds told him stories, of big juicy pies,
While squirrels did yoga beneath swirling skies.

With an orange in slippers, they danced on the grass,
While shadows of apples watched the fun pass.
But a pear tripped on laughter and fell with a thud,
Just like the giggles that rolled down like flood!

## Stories Weaved in Petals

In a garden of winks and giggles,
Petals hum tunes of silly jiggles.
Bumblebees dance in quirky pairs,
While butterflies argue without any cares.

Grapes gossip low about the sun,
While tree trunks laugh, 'Oh, what fun!'
The carrots wear hats, think they're all cool,
As radishes prank like they're in school.

Under the sky, they make a scene,
With fruit so bright, like a jellybean.
Each harvest ripe with tales to tell,
And every fruit wishes you well.

## From Seed to Sweetness

A tiny seed once had a dream,
To grow up big and join the team.
It stretched and yawned beneath the dirt,
And popped up wearing a leafy shirt.

Tomatoes boast of their red parade,
While squashes play hide and seek in shade.
Peas start rolling, laughing with glee,
'We're in pods, not just in a spree!'

Bananas giggle, oh what a sight,
Stumbling down, they slip out of fright.
Each fruit and veg in hilarious chase,
In this yard, they find their place.

## **Glistening Dreams in Every Bite**

Apples shine bright, like little moons,
As squirrels hum silly, silly tunes.
Pineapples wear crowns, quite the jest,
While oranges roll, 'We're the zest!'

Berries tease with bursts of cheer,
Whisper sweet secrets, oh so near.
With every nibble, laughter flows,
Crisp lettuce shouts, 'Hey, let's pose!'

For every crunch, there's a giggle too,
Food so funny, it's good for you.
In every bite, dreams ignite,
With each munch, the world feels right.

## Underneath the Canopy of Green

The leaves above shimmy, sway, and twist,
While the apples giggle, 'We can't be missed!'
Under mighty branches, creatures play,
Finding new games with every sway.

Nuts chat softly, 'What's your plan?'
As strawberries argue, 'I'm the best in the clan!'
The sun sneaks peeks through foliage tight,
Casting shadows that dance in delight.

With laughter afloat, and friendship ripe,
Everyone sings to the gardener's hype.
Joy blooms wild in this bountiful scene,
As shadows stretch long in the evening green.

## **Serendipity in Every Bite**

A pear danced with a cheeky peach,
They giggled as they rolled on the beach.
An apple shouted, 'Hey, come and see!'
But the banana slipped and fell with glee.

The grapes are plotting a fruity coup,
While strawberries wear hats that are blue.
A melon jokes, 'I'm the pick of the patch!'
And cherries blush with the sweetest catch.

## Petals and Promise

The daisies wore hats made of dew,
While tulips tossed petals and flew.
Roses tried dancing but tripped on a stem,
'Next time, let's stick to a gentlehem!'

Butterflies laughed, caught in the fray,
As violets chimed in with a 'yippee!' hooray.
Lilies debated on which shade to wear,
The sunflowers shrugged, 'We don't even care!'

## Tapestry of Flavor

A fig and a lemon played tag in the sun,
Together they laughed just having some fun.
A raspberry rolled, almost went splat,
'Watch out!' cried the kiwi, 'You might get flat!'

Their laughter blended like a sweet song,
In the kitchen, they all danced along.
Berries bursting, juicy and bright,
They cheered for the day that felt just right.

## A Symphony of Seasons

Autumn's apples threw a big party,
While winter pears dressed all snazzy and hearty.
Spring's blossoms burst forth with flair,
While summer's fruits sprawled everywhere!

The seasons jammed in a fruity band,
With a beat that was perfectly unplanned.
Each bite a note, each flavor a rhyme,
To the rhythm of nature, oh, what a time!

## Nectar of Nature's Breach

In the grove where laughter grows,
Bees dance with nectar, sweet as prose.
Fruit spills over in comical heaps,
As squirrels plan heists, giggling in leaps.

With plump pears thinking they're quite the catch,
They dodge rolls of fur like a misplaced patch.
Yet cider's there, giving us cheer,
As the fruits collaborate, 'Let's get some beer!'

## Autumn's Hand on Tender Leaves

Leaves tumble down like a confetti show,
Each hiding a tale, sous-chef to the low.
Pumpkin's cheeks are all aglow,
While ghosts sneak by with too much dough.

Goblins giggle in the fading light,
Trading acorns for a taste of fright.
Autumn winks, with a wink that's sly,
As the bounty turns into dessert pie.

## Apples and Shadows in Soft Sunlight

In a patch of sun, apples dance with glee,
Winking at shadows, making quite a spree.
One applesauce thought, 'I'm way too sweet!'
While others debate who's more ripe to eat.

A shadow quips, 'I'm cooler by day,'
'But when night falls, I'll lead the way!'
They chuckle and tumble, in playful delight,
As the taste of fun turns the day into night.

## Roots of Abundance

In the soil where jokes grow deep,
Roots twist and wiggle, not wanting to sleep.
Grapes snicker as they plan their wine,
'We're the grape-est, and that's just fine!'

Meanwhile, the carrots are plotting a race,
To see who can sprout with the fastest pace.
They laugh and they tumble as life's little jest,
In a garden where every plant is blessed.

## A Symphony of Harvest

With apples on the ground, they dance,
The pears are doing a wobbly prance.
A cantaloupe wore a silly hat,
While oranges rolled like a playful cat.

Grapes giggle as they bounce on the vine,
Watermelons plotting on how to dine.
Peaches twirl in a fruity ballet,
While cherries laugh and yell, "We're on our way!"

The wind plays a tune, oh what a sight,
As pumpkins bounce into the night.
With every fruit, a joke indeed,
In this garden of laughter, there's plenty to feed.

So grab a slice and take a bite,
These fruits bring laughter, pure delight.
In the harvest of joy, we find the fun,
A fruity festival for everyone!

## Enchanted in Sunlight and Shade

In tangled vines where shadows play,
Tomatoes blush at the end of the day.
Zucchini make hats with leaves so wide,
While bell peppers play hide-and-seek with pride.

Squash giggles as it tumbles down,
Eggplants wear dresses and spin around.
Broccoli crowns like kings of the patch,
While radishes munch on a leafy batch.

Carrots stick out their orange noses,
In hopes a bunny will come and doze.
The cornstands tall in lines of cheer,
As butterflies flit, spreading joy near.

So come and enjoy this magical space,
Where veggies are funny and share their grace.
In sunlight and shade, they bloom and thrive,
In this garden of laughs, we're all alive!

## Legacies of the Branches

From branches low, a pear dropped down,
A mischievous giggle, it wore a frown.
Cherries chatted, planning a scheme,
While bananas whispered, "Let's chase a dream!"

The old apple tree creaked with glee,
Old jokes resurfaced like a comedy spree.
Coconuts laughed, "We're hard on the shell,
But fruit friends, we're just full of swell!"

The breezy laughter filled the air,
As funny tales flew everywhere.
Grapefruits bounced with a jazz-like flair,
In a game of tag with no one aware.

Among the branches, hilarity grows,
Every fruit with a tale it knows.
A legacy built on laughter and cheer,
In this fruity family, joy's always near!

## Harvesting Hope

In gardens lush, where laughter thrives,
Old pumpkins tell tales of their lives.
While rhubarb snickers "Oh what a fright!
No one picked me for the pie tonight!"

Peas in pods create a chatty crew,
Sprouting dreams of a veggie stew.
Cabbages roll like fluffy balls,
While onions hide from the autumn squalls.

Each harvest brings a playful jest,
In each plump fruit, a hidden quest.
Vegetables beam with a comical glow,
Ready to share their tales as they grow.

So, join the fun in this bountiful land,
With veggies and fruits all hand in hand.
For in harvesting hope, we find our way,
A funny fresh feast, come gather and play!

## The Cartographer of Fruits

I drew a map of apples and pears,
Guided by laughter and silly stares.
Bananas giggled in their bright yellow hue,
While oranges rolled away, not knowing what to do.

The cherries conspired, oh what a sight,
Plotting their mischief under the moonlight.
Peaches wore hats, looking quite dapper,
Pineapples danced, making others a snapper.

My fruit-filled map, what a whimsical find,
Each curve and each turn, a joy intertwined.
With lemons erupting in zesty delight,
It's a fruity adventure, a real tasty bite.

So here's to the fruits, with their antics and cheer,
A cartographer's life, oh how could I steer?
Each scribble and doodle brings laughter so bright,
In the world of fruits, everything feels right.

## Captured in Each Succulent Bite

Strawberries blushed like they could not hide,
In the jam jar, they cheered for a ride.
Melons whispered secrets, sweet and absurd,
Each slice a giggle, not to be disturbed.

I took a bite out of a funny old pear,
It chuckled back, 'You just can't compare!'
With nectarines juggling in playful glee,
Each piece of fruit sings, 'Come laugh with me!'

Grapes get together, a rowdy embrace,
Their skins burst open, oh what a race!
At the picnic table, they plot to unite,
Mischief in every single juicy bite.

So feast on their humor, fresh and divine,
Each morsel's a tickle, a sweet merry line.
Captured in moments of sweet, silly cheer,
A banquet of laughter, year after year.

## Sweet Reminiscing Underneath the Trees

We lounged in the shade of the apple tree's sway,
With whispers of fruit games, we laughed the day away.
Pears told grand tales of their lofty fall,
While plump apricots boasted of their juicy all.

The oranges rumbled, 'We've got zest to share!'
As berries chimed in with stylish flair.
With each passing breeze, stories took flight,
Moments of sweetness in the golden light.

The figs chimed in, 'We've no time to waste,
Let's ponder our flavors—oh, what a taste!'
Underneath moonbeams, we giggled and swayed,
Remembering bites where every joke played.

So here's to those evenings, sweet as can be,
Beneath fruit-laden branches, so carefree.
With laughter as ripples in the soft twilight,
Like a slice of a pie, everything feels right.

## The Poetry of Growth

Seeds were laughing when they took a stretch,
Poking up softly, like 'What's the catch?'
Sprouts began telling their tall tales of woe,
As snails in the garden planned their slow show.

The vegetables joined with their leafy cheer,
'We'll sprout some jokes, so come lend an ear!'
With radishes bold and cucumbers bright,
They plotted and danced, a silly delight.

Every blossom had something funny to share,
From lilies to daisies, making us stare.
A garden so quirky, with a life all its own,
In this patch of humor, laughter has grown.

So here's to the rhythm of growth all around,
In the soil, in the sun, where joy can be found.
The poetry of plants, with their comical spins,
Brings smiles and sweet chuckles, wherever it begins.

## Embrace of Roots and Rains

Underneath, the roots do wiggle,
Tickling toes, making us giggle.
Rainy days bring droppy cheer,
Splashing puddles, never fear!

We dance around in muddy glee,
Who knew roots could be so free?
They wrap us up in a leafy hug,
Then laugh with us, the soggy smug!

So here we stand, a silly sight,
With drippy hats, oh what a fright!
Yet all around, so much delight,
Nature's joy, our hearts take flight!

So let it rain, let roots entwine,
For in this mess, all things align.
We'll splash and trip, then laugh aloud,
With nature's gifts, we are truly proud!

## Quiet Beneath the Leaves


Amidst the rustle, whispers play,
The leaves gossip, come what may.
They tease the squirrels, call them names,
While hiding acorns, oh such games!

Beneath the shade, we lay and dream,
Imagining things that burst and gleam.
What if the branches could tell tales?
Of jovial robins and silly snails?

A breezy giggle, a soft embrace,
Nature's humor fills the space.
A laugh escapes, a sigh of bliss,
Beneath the leaves, we can't miss!

So let us drift in leafy shade,
And join the fun that sunshine made.
In every rustle, laughter weaves,
A secret world beneath the leaves!

## Beneath the Bounty

Fruits are ripe and hanging low,
A feast awaits, now let's have a show!
Tomatoes juggle, apples tease,
It's fruity chaos, oh please, oh please!

Beneath this bounty, we can munch,
The berry brigade throws a fruit punch!
Lemons giggle, plums in a race,
Citrus smiles plastered on the face!

Peaches stumble, pears take a bow,
Oh, what a fruity fun-row!
With every bite, a merry dance,
Under the trees, we prance and prance!

So gather 'round, it's harvest time,
Let nature's jokes become our rhyme.
Beneath this pile of fresh delight,
We find our laughter, pure as light!

## **Cradling Nature's Treasure**

Hidden gems in every nook,
A treasure map of greenish book.
The potatoes hide, they play in dirt,
While carrots peek, without a shirt!

We unearth laughter, plants surprise,
Broccoli crowns, a chef's disguise.
Radishes giggle, onions weep,
In this garden, joy runs deep!

Tomatoes wobble, a funny sight,
With every pluck, the world feels right.
We cradle nature's quirky greens,
In every twist, a chuckle beams!

So let us dig and dance around,
In this treasure, mirth is found.
With muddy hands and silly treasure,
Our hearts are light with simple pleasure!

## Where Whimsy Meets Harvest

In a patch of apples, bright and bold,
A squirrel claimed them, oh so uncontrolled.
He danced and twirled, a fruity spree,
As berries laughed, saying, "Look at he!"

With every nibble, he grew quite round,
The leaves whispered, "What's lost can be found!"
His acorn cap crooked, a crown of cheese,
He ruled this orchard with buried pleas.

## The Legacy of Luscious Trees

In rows of trees, not one stood still,
Bananas giggled, what a bitter thrill.
They swung their peels in zany delight,
And avocados plotted all through the night.

A grape climbed high, to brag and boast,
"Who needs a ladder when I'm your host?"
But slipped on juice, and down he fell,
Laughing fruits cried, "That was swell!"

## In the Shade of Abundance

Under leafy umbrellas, the fruit brigade,
Pineapples lounged, wearing shades well-laid.
While plums organized a sit-down feast,
With lime and lemon, grilled up a beast!

The watermelon cracked jokes all day,
"Why so melon-choly? Let's play, hey, hey!"
The cantaloupe burst forth with laughter,
"Next time, let's skip the fruities after!"

## Resilient as the Thicket

Among the brambles, a berry spun tales,
Of daring escapes, and wild delivery fails.
Beneath the thicket, where chaos churned,
They laughed and rolled, for joy was earned.

A raspberry proclaimed, "I'm quite the bard,"
As nuts joined in, no reason to guard.
With every twist, humor flew high,
A jester's fruit fair, beneath the sky.

## Shadows of Sweetness

In the grove where fruit does hang,
A squirrel danced, and then he sang.
He tripped on grapes and went headfirst,
A laugh erupted, oh how it burst!

The cherries giggled on their stem,
As bees played tag, what a mayhem!
One flew too close, got a surprise,
The peach said, 'Hey, watch where you fly!'

Underneath the lemon tree shade,
The rascals plotted, plans they made.
To steal a bite, what a relief,
Till the dog barked, and then, disbelief!

A watermelon wore shades so cool,
While cantaloupes played in a pool.
The blossoms blushed, so full of charm,
As laughter echoed, their sweet alarm!

## Lush Abundance in Sunlit Glades

In the light where berries sway,
A rabbit danced his clumsy ballet.
He bounced and rolled, just like a pro,
Till he tripped on an orange—oh no, no, no!

The apples chuckled, bright and round,
As pears fell down without a sound.
One landed on a snail's back slow,
They shrugged and grinned, 'A tasty show!'

The sunlit glades are full of cheer,
While giggling fruits draw near and near.
The laughter swells with every breeze,
As plums engage in fruit-themed tease!

Green vines dance, all tangled tight,
With cucumbers hiding in plain sight.
Oh what a scene, so wild, absurd,
As nature's jokes fly free as birds!

**Echoes of Nature's Bounty**

In the field where laughter flows,
Tomatoes wear silly hats, I suppose.
With each ripe giggle, they roll about,
The farmer joins in, vibrating with doubt!

Cabbages plot in leafy disguise,
While the radishes swap funny lies.
A turnip painted like a clown,
Brought all the veggies tumbling down!

Beneath the trees, in playful rings,
The garlic clapped, it pulled some strings.
Each crunch a melody in the air,
As onions cried, "We smell beyond compare!"

With carrots leaping, oh what a sight,
They formed a band to celebrate night.
Amidst the harvest, small joys are found,
Echoes of laughter, all around!

# A Tapestry of Blossoms

In a garden where the tulips sway,
A dandelion tried to join the play.
But when it bounced, it lost its fluff,
"Oh dear! No more of that, it's tough!"

The daisies laughed in the morning sun,
As bees waltzed by just having fun.
A lily, elegant, struck a pose,
Then tripped on a stem—what a rose!

With every bloom, the jesters cheer,
The violets whisper, "Grab a beer!"
As petals float like confetti bright,
The garden parties go all night!

Amongst the color, laughter grows,
In this tapestry, joy overflows.
Each flower shares a funny tale,
In nature's court, we cannot fail!

## The Woven Tapestry of Life

Apples dangle on a thread,
Hanging tight, they play in dread.
"Catch me, catch me!" they all scream,
As fruit flies dart, a silly dream.

Peaches blush in tree-top chats,
Whispers shared from furry brats.
"Who's the juiciest?" asks the plum,
While pears just giggle, feeling glum.

Cherries bounce with laughter loud,
A raucous, silly, fruity crowd.
Beneath the leaves, they throw a bash,
Their giggles bright as summer's flash.

So let's toast to juicy glee,
In this wild, sweet jubilee.
Life's a dance on nature's stage,
With fruit-filled fun, we turn the page.

## Beneath the Golden Sun

Lemons frown with sunny zest,
Sour faces, putting patience to the test.
"Hey, squeeze me!" calls the grape with glee,
While orange rolls beneath a tree.

Beneath the rays, the berries pry,
Lamenting how they just can't fly.
"Let's form a team!" the blackberries shout,
While sesame seeds just stroll about.

Bananas slip with giggles and gaffes,
In a game of tag, they split their halves.
They whizzed past trees with slippery care,
Yelling, "Watch out! We've got flair!"

So we laugh at nature's tricks,
With tangy jokes and playful kicks.
Under the sun's warm, glowing fun,
We embrace the fruit, each little pun.

## When Nature Speaks Softly

Breezes whisper through bright vines,
Telling tales of silly signs.
Fruits converse with gentle grace,
As they bounce from place to place.

"Who's the silliest?" asks the fig,
While peers giggle with every jig.
"I'm the tastiest!" says the peach,
Then drops down without a breach.

Tomatoes blush, their secret shared,
"Don't slice too deep; please handle with care!"
Carrots dance, their tops askew,
"Let's show the world what we can do!"

When nature chuckles, all are keen,
Fruitful plays amidst the green.
With laughter floating in each breeze,
It's a funny tale with fruit as keys.

## Vestiges of a Summer Gone

Leaves have turned a crispy hue,
As apples share their autumn view.
"Oh no," said one, "this season's rough,"
While pumpkins laugh, "Ain't it tough?"

Ciders poured with foamy cheer,
Forgettable memories draw near.
"Remember summer?" said the pear,
"Those lazy days? We had a scare!"

Yet winters bloom with frosty glee,
"Might as well chill, let it be free!"
Nuts prepare for silly fights,
Making snowballs on cozy nights.

So let's smile at summer's play,
Recalling fruits with zestful sway.
Though time rolls on with its swiftness,
The fun lingers in its fitness.

## The Taste of Time's Tenderness

In the orchard where apples swing,
A squirrel stole a pie, what a thing!
When life hands you fruit, make a fuss,
But the bird stole the pie—what a plus!

With every bite, giggles ensue,
Oh, the odd things that fruit can do!
A peach in my pocket, oh what a sight,
Just don't ask me to share, that's a fight!

Grapes like marbles roll in a race,
Bouncing 'round the trees at a furious pace.
Raccoons in tuxedos, oh what a scene,
Stealing snacks like royalty, you know what I mean!

So, here's to the bounty, let's raise a cheer,
For every silly moment shared this year.
The fruit may be sweet, the laughter divine,
In this whimsically wacky, fruity design!

**Blooming Joy in Every Season.**

The flowers giggle in the spring light,
A bee bumps the bloom, oh what a fright!
Daisy chains made of laughter galore,
Combine it with sunshine, who could ask for more?

In summer's heat, we chase butterflies,
While the watermelon wears a clever disguise.
Sipping lemonade under a tree,
A lemonade stand led by a bumblebee!

Autumn leaves dance while pumpkins grin,
A raccoon plays dress-up, and sports a pin!
Chasing after acorns, the funniest sight,
When squirrels in suits act like it's a night!

Winter wraps in a frosty cape,
Snowmen giggle as raindrops escape.
With cocoa in hand, we warm our hearts,
In every season, laughter imparts!

## Harvested Whispers

Under the trees, where the secrets grow,
A worm sings praises—how does he know?
With every harvest, giggling ensues,
Cuz who knew tomatoes could wear little shoes?

Carrots in wigs dance the night away,
While radishes joke about the fray.
Potatoes tell tales, all lumpy and grand,
Of an ancient kingdom, where vegetables planned!

Election time comes for the corn and beans,
A battle to win for the freshest greens.
In this veggie saga, oh what a split,
As peas throw confetti—each one a hit!

So join in the fun, let your laughter out,
In fields of whispers where veggies shout.
The treasures we harvest, like joy, we find,
In rhymes of the garden, where friendship's entwined!

## Secrets Beneath the Boughs

Beneath the branches, a secret spree,
The critters gather for tea with glee.
Mice in bowties sip their fine brew,
While the fox plays waiter, just for a view!

The pears hold court, discussing the day,
While mushrooms forget what they meant to say.
Chirps and giggles weave through the leaves,
As gossip flows like the warm summer breeze.

A hedgehog reveals a dance on the grass,
While rabbits flip-flop, just a tad crass.
Each secret exchanged is a chuckle, a smile,
A community built, even if just for a while!

So come by the boughs, where laughter runs free,
The best stories told are under the tree.
In the heart of the grove, friendships abound,
With secrets and laughter in whispers resound!

# A Patchwork of Blossoms

In the garden, apples play,
Dancing on the branch all day.
Cherries giggle, pears make a fuss,
While bananas plot to ride the bus.

Peaches prance in petal hats,
Lemons laugh at silly chats.
Grapes attempt a conga line,
But plums just want to sip their wine.

Nuts are cracking jokes so loud,
While berries try to form a crowd.
Each fruit brings a comic twist,
In this fruity frolic, none are missed.

With every bloom, a silly tale,
Of veggie bands and spicy ale.
A patchwork of colors in the sun,
Where laughter ripens, and all have fun.

## Nature's Silent Offering

The tulips whisper in the breeze,
While daisies giggle at the bees.
Roses wink as thorns play fair,
And daisies don a floral pair.

Morning glories stretch and yawn,
A comical show at the break of dawn.
Each flower tells a secret pun,
In the garden where laughter's spun.

The bees buzz jokes and share their views,
While butterflies wear colorful shoes.
A silent offering, yet so loud,
With petals bowing, proud and wowed.

It's a carnival of scents and sights,
With a merry mix of day and nights.
Nature's humor fills every space,
In this funny, floral, happy place.

## Where Darkness Meets Fruition

Amidst the shadows, fruits awake,
In hidden corners, they burst and shake.
Bitter melons wear frowns so deep,
While coconuts dance, ready to leap.

Pumpkins plot in midnight glee,
Turning lanterns, oh so free!
Eggplants grin, so purple bold,
Whispering tales of magic told.

Wombats rave at the harvest feast,
While mushrooms sport capes, oh what a beast!
Each stash of goodies, a joke to tell,
As darkness meets joy, all's going well.

From peaches to plums, with smiles to share,
Fruition blooms in the cool night air.
In this silly world of dark and light,
Laughter grows in the hush of night.

## On the Feast of Fallen Fruits

When fruits fall down, they start to roll,
A wild parade, a comical stroll.
Peppers jive in a veggie dream,
While oranges plot a zesty scheme.

Grasshoppers join the fray with glee,
Squirrels skewer jokes like brie.
Ripe tomatoes toss in rivalry,
While melons laugh with sheer jubilee.

Festivities rise on leafy greens,
As nature's bounty shares its scenes.
Pumpkin pies take center stage,
As fruits bow down for the next page.

A feast for all, with laughter spread,
As fruity jokes dance in our head.
On this playful day of fun, we cheer,
For every fruit that brings us near.

## Cherished Abundance in the Air

In the garden where fruits swing low,
Laughter dances where the wild winds blow.
Apples tumble with a playful thud,
While goofy squirrels slip into the mud.

Bananas chuckle, wearing peels like hats,
Strawberries giggle at the jumpy rats.
Ripe melons roll in a fat, jolly race,
Though grapes sometimes trip, they still keep pace.

## Resonance of Ripe Silence

Peaches whisper secrets of juicy delight,
They laugh at the sun, glowing bold and bright.
Cherries flirt, swinging with blissful glee,
While plums defy gravity, how can that be?

The citrus sing songs of zesty surprise,
Jokes shared with bees buzzing 'round their fries.
Each fruit unpeels a story so sweet,
In this fruity party, no one's discreet!

## A Riddle of Seeds

Seeds planted deep in the soil's warm womb,
Wondering when they'll escape from the gloom.
They crack up in laughter as sprouts push through,
Telling old tales of what seeds ought to do!

The carrots wear glasses, the radishes blush,
While cucumbers hop in a worried rush.
"Am I a fruit or a veggie?" they ask,
In this leafy domain, all face the same task.

## **Flavors of the Past**

Old trees recall tales of summers gone by,
Sharing sweet whispers with wind fluttering high.
Memories linger in the ripe fruits so bright,
As the berries paint stories under the light.

Fruits dressed up in folklore, vibrant and bold,
Telling of winters and stories retold.
A playful wind tickles across every branch,
As flavors of laughter take a fruity chance.

# Melodies from Hidden Delights

In the breeze, a laugh takes flight,
Where juicy dreams blend day and night.
The apples giggle, the pears they dance,
Nature's tunes put doubt in a trance.

Dancing squirrels steal a quick bite,
Bouncing around, what a silly sight!
While bees hum tunes that sound quite sweet,
Nature's concert, a hilarious treat.

Cherries blush, thinking they're shy,
While lemons break into a pie in the sky.
With laughter in every rusty breeze,
The fruit on the trees just aims to please.

Robins join in, with a cheeky chirp,
While pondering why the worms will burp.
Oranges roll down with a sunny plan,
Leaving giggles where the fun began.

## Gifts Wrapped in Nature's Caress

Beneath the leaves, a treasure hides,
Wrapped in laughter, where giggles bide.
An acorn's nutty joke makes rounds,
As rabbits chuckle without any bounds.

Each berry winks, a cheeky tease,
As daisies dance with a gentle breeze.
Nature's gifts bring joy galore,
Even frogs croak, "We're all hardcore!"

The sun shines bright, teasing the moon,
A game of hide-and-seek, they swoon.
While veggies play dress-up in the dirt,
Carrots wear hats, it's quite the flirt!

In shadows, gifts begin to bloom,
With laughter spilling from each radish room.
A riot of colors in nature's frame,
Every moment feels like a merry game.

## Conversations with the Oldest Trees

With gnarled roots and stories bold,
The trees all chuckle, their tales unfold.
"Have you seen the fruit take flight?"
"Only when they're caught in delight!"

Branches gossip in the afternoon sun,
Whispering secrets of nature's fun.
"Last week, a squirrel made quite a fuss,
Claiming he found a flying bus!"

Leaves tickle the air, like old pals would,
"Remember the time, we all knocked wood?"
The trunks shake with laughter, creaking so loud,
In a forest where joy's in every cloud.

Old trees chuckle, they've seen it all,
From caterpillar thoughts to autumn's call.
Life's merry pranks leave them in glee,
As they settle down for a grand jubilee.

## Salutations from the Ground Below

Down below where the beetles play,
The soil's alive with a comical sway.
"Mushrooms say hi with a tip of their cap,
While worms orchestrate the funniest rap!"

"Do you hear that giggle, right under your feet?
It's the garden fairies having a meet!"
With shovels and trowels, they dance in their glee,
Even the radishes join the jubilee.

Gravel chuckles as weeds weave a tale,
"Life's so much better when you set your sail!"
And the roots bow low, like they own the show,
Celebrating each little seedling that grows.

The ground is a stage for comedic flair,
With moments of joy floating in the air.
Every sprout's laughter weaves wondrous spells,
As nature's winks ring in joyful bells.

# The Sweet Weight of Waiting

Sitting in the shade, it's time to eat,
My fruit is ripe, oh what a treat!
But first I must wait, here's the catch,
For squirrels to sneak in and make a swatch.

I chase them away, with a loud yell,
They giggle and scamper, oh what the hell!
I sit like a statue, my arms crossed tight,
While squirrels plot raucous in broad daylight.

The wind starts to blow, my hat flies away,
Chasing after it, oh what a day!
The fruit drops down, right into my lap,
Now I'm a target for nature's own trap!

With pie plans postponed and patience wore thin,
I laugh at the chaos, let merriment win.
These moments of mischief are quite the show,
Who knew nature's antics could steal the show?

# Remnants of Sun-drenched Days

The sun was relentless, on that sizzling day,
I thought I'd find apples, but alas, no way!
Just a few bruised ones, in grass they lay,
I pondered a snack, then heard a goat bray.

"Hey, that's mine!" I yelled, in a playful rage,
The goat munches apples, set loose from a cage.
He chews with a grin, no guilt in his face,
As I plan my next move, with some style and grace.

I finally snatch fruit, a glorious sight,
But it's loaded with worms; oh, what a fright!
Yet I slice it all thin, with laughter anew,
A feast for the ants—at least they're not blue!

Such are the treasures that summer can yield,
Not all that we hope for, but laughter's the shield.
Even with wormy treats and goats on the prowl,
I relish each moment, with a chuckle and howl!

## Picking the Past

I wandered the rows, with basket in hand,
Remembering days of fruit pie-making grand.
But all I can find are memories bright,
And a few shriveled figs that don't taste right.

I spot an old tree, its fruit looking fine,
But alas, it's a memory—fruits of time.
With every pluck, a story unfolds,
Of laughter and mishaps and tales that are bold.

Turns out the tree is a little unfit,
It offers me visions, but not a single bit!
I laugh at the ghosts that play peek-a-boo,
As I haul away leaves—what else can I do?

In this orchard of wisdom, I chuckle, I sigh,
For the past has its laughter, and memories fly.
With every shake, a chuckle, a grin,
Picking my laughter, is where I begin!

## **A Tangle of Roots**

Beneath my feet lies a twisty dread,
With roots that seem more like a creature's head.
I stumble and trip over nature's own game,
As vines try to anchor me, calling my name.

"Come join us," they whisper, a mischievous tone,
"Let's pull you down here, you'll never be alone!"
With twigs in my hair and dirt on my face,
I wonder how long I could last in this space.

I laugh at the chaos, this jungle of fun,
These roots are a challenge, a daring run.
With every step forward, I give quite a show,
An acrobat's dance on the orchard's own flow!

But I've met my match, the roots are too sly,
They tangle my feet, and I'm stuck; oh my!
I'll take these wild moments, forever enshrined,
For in every stumble, there's laughter designed!

## Fruits of Forgotten Dreams

In the garden of my mind, there's a tree,
It grows sweet thoughts left behind by me.
Each fruit has a face, a giggle or two,
They laugh as they ripen, what else can they do?

Bananas in pajamas, all peeking about,
Their slippery dance moves, they're hard to doubt.
An apple wearing glasses, so wise and so grand,
Says, "Trust in the fruit, it's all part of the plan!"

The cherries are gossiping, full of delight,
Trading all secrets on a warm summer night.
While peaches in fluff, with fluffiest smiles,
Chase after the plums for a game of old styles.

So here's to the thoughts that once took their flight,
Fruitful reminders of what feels so light.
In laughter we find what was lost in the haze,
In the boughs of our dreams, where the funny fruit plays.

## **Nectar of the Season**

Honey drips down like a comical joke,
The bees are all buzzing, oh what a bloke!
With nectar so sticky, they've loaded their packs,
Creating sweet chaos, not just in their snacks.

A citrus parade, oh what a scene,
Lemons in tutus, so fancy and keen.
They dance in a circle, all shimmery bright,
While limes wear top hats, just feeling the light.

Grapes play the banjo, strumming real slow,
They've got silly rhythms that steal the show.
With each little pluck, they burst into cheer,
A jolly good time, come gather, my dear!

In this season of laughter, let's drink it all in,
With fruity concoctions, we're surely to win.
Raise a glass to the nectar with bubbles that pop,
In a world full of laughter, we just can't stop!

## **Blooming Beneath the Canopy**

Under the leaves, a gathering's set,
Flowers hold meetings we can't quite forget.
Daisies debate on how tall they can grow,
While sunflowers grin, basking in golden glow.

Petunias wear shades, sipping dew with a flair,
They're plotting a heist, it's only fair.
With vines all around forming a lazy maze,
They giggle about in their colorful ways.

The tulips play tag with a light summer breeze,
While daisies spin round, trying hard not to sneeze.
The poppies make jokes about needing more sun,
In this flowery circus, there's laughter for fun!

Under the canopy, where humor's the seed,
These blooms start a festival, a floral creed.
Each petal a story, they bloom, twist and bend,
In laughter's embrace, let the fun never end!

## Apples of Time's Embrace

In the orchard of wishes, an apple did land,
Its skin told a tale, a comical brand.
With wrinkled old laughter and stories to share,
It chuckled with time, 'You ought to beware!'

A fork in the road turned into a fruit,
The laughter grew louder from each little root.
They whispered of seasons, of moments gone by,
While pears joined the rhythm with a wink in their eye.

"Oh, remember the time we got lost in a pie?"
An apple exclaimed with a gleam in the eye.
"Or the pear who got stuck in a tree upside-down,
Spent hours in stitches, an upside-down clown!"

So let us all savor these tales of delight,
With apples of time, let's step into night.
In each juicy bite, there's a giggle that stays,
Wrapped in sweet memories, life's funny little ways.

## **Bounty Beneath the Blossoms**

Underneath the blooming trees,
A squirrel dances with such ease.
He grabs a pear, but oops! It slips,
And lands right on his tiny lips!

The apples giggle, ripe and round,
As he scrambles on the ground.
With every hop, the branches sway,
"Hey, no stealing! We're on display!"

The cherries blush, a bright red glow,
While strawberries whisper, "Watch the show!"
A watermelon rolls, a sight so grand,
As everyone joins this merry band.

Beneath the blooms, they frolic free,
In a fruity comedy spree!
With laughter sweet as summer's kiss,
Nature's bounty brings such bliss!

## **Harvest Moon's Embrace**

The moon peeks in with a cheeky grin,
As pumpkins ponder where to begin.
One claims he's the fairest of all,
While a cabbage shouts, "Look! I'm tall!"

Corn stalks gossip, swaying their tops,
"Did you hear? Last week he dropped!"
A carrot snickers, well-rooted and keen,
As they plot their next Halloween scene.

The moonlight dances on fruits and greens,
As veggies plot in ridiculous schemes.
With a wink and a wave, they plot their shows,
Each one wild, as the laughter grows.

So beneath that big old harvest moon,
The garden sings a silly tune.
In the still of night, under stars so bright,
The critters share their comedic light!

## **Whispers of Ripening Fruits**

In the treetop, apples plot and scheme,
With tales of pies that make us scream.
A peach chimes in with a juicy boast,
"Just wait until I'm served as toast!"

Berries chuckle in a juicy crowd,
As their sweetness swells, oh so proud.
A banana slips with a goofy grin,
"C'mon, let's dance! Who's joining in?"

The grapes are rolling, round and round,
While lemons frown at the silly sound.
A fruit salad waits for its big debut,
Mixing laughter with sunshine too!

So here they are, the merry bunch,
Sharing smiles over a fruity lunch.
As the sun sets, they dream of delight,
In the whispers of the coming night!

## Secrets Held in Twisted Branches

In twisted limbs, they scheme away,
As nuts and fruits come out to play.
"Do you hear?" one pear whispers bright,
"There's a party under the moonlight!"

Ripe figs giggle with secret glee,
While a tomato grins, "Look at me!"
Branches bend with every cheer,
As they toast to laughter, loud and clear.

"They think we hang here without a care,
But we've got antics; let's make them stare!"
An orange spins, a citrus ballet,
While coconuts laugh, "Just watch them sway!"

Under the stars, so wild and free,
A fruit fiesta unfolds on the tree.
With whispers, giggles, and silly pranks,
They toast with juice—"Thanks for the flanks!"

## **A Lullaby of Fruitful Whispers**

In the shade, a pear turned pink,
Said to the apple, "Let's not overthink!"
They giggled softly, tension-free,
As peaches danced with bumblebee.

A lemon sighed in zestful cheer,
"Why does the grapefruit always sneer?"
A berry blushed, all plump and round,
"Let's squeeze some joy from underground!"

When cherries told their cautionary tales,
Of squirrels stealing their little trails,
Laughter broke through every laughable leaf,
As nature spun a web of joy, no grief.

So hush now, fruits, take flight,
With each giggle, we delight!
Beneath the sky, a vibrant crew,
In fruity whispers, friendship grew.

## Beneath the Canopy of Giving

Underneath the boughs, a funny duck,
Complained about the kiwi's luck.
"Why am I stuck with just plain mud?"
While bananas giggled in a flood!

The orange chuckled, bright and round,
"At least you're not the one that's browned!"
Avocados rapped, green and slick,
"A salad's where we blend our trick!"

A melon's joke was deemed too ripe,
"I'm feeling like a fruity type!"
With every pun, the gaggle cheered,
Their juicy tales are highly revered!

So under leaves so lush and wide,
These giggling fruits took joy in stride.
From every branch, a chuckle sprung,
In clever chords, their song was sung.

## Threads of Sun and Soil

In the sun, a cantaloupe sighed,
"Why must I sit! Oh, this is fried!"
A grape replied, "Not so austere,
At least you're sweet, my dear!"

The strawberries stitched a blanket bright,
"Shall we share this fruity delight?"
While the radish tried to play along,
"My roots are deep, I'll join this throng!"

As pomegranates burst with zest,
"We've got to be the very best!"
A fig chimed in, full of flair,
"Let's wrap it up, but with some care!"

With giggles sewn through grassy seams,
The fruits of life spun sunny dreams.
They crafted fun with every thread,
A tapestry of laughs ahead!

## Echoes of Lush Gatherings

In the grove, a silly peach exclaimed,
"Why are we all so unashamed?"
The plums rolled eyes, their skin so bold,
"We're fabulous, or so we're told!"

A pineapple tossed a spiky grin,
"Am I the queen, or just a sin?"
Bananas slipped and took a dive,
"In this crowd, we're all alive!"

The figs threw glitter over grass,
"Let's make this a fruit-flavored sass!"
As lemons buzzed their citrus jokes,
Laughter rippled through the folks.

So raised a toast, with juice and cheer,
To friendships forged in every sphere.
In nature's laughter, they felt free,
Echoes of mirth, forever be!

## Bountiful Conversations at Dusk

In evening light, the apples grin,
They're plotting pranks, let the games begin.
Pears giggle softly, ripe with jest,
As pumpkins crown the hen's jesting fest.

The laughter swells like cider's brew,
Chasing the shadows, just me and you.
Strawberries whisper juicy delight,
While carrots twirl in their leafy flight.

Squirrels toss acorns, in wild display,
"Who needs a winter? Let's party today!"
The corn stalks dance, in a swaying spree,
Even the weeds join, "Come sing with me!"

Under the stars, our voices collide,
With fruit and folly, there's nothing to hide.
Mirth and mayhem in the dusky air,
A carnival blooms, all fruit have a share.

## An Ode to Autumn's Embrace

Oh crimson leaves, like clowns on the run,
With every gust, they frolic and spun.
Nutty acorns take flight like a dart,
While chestnuts gather, laughing from the start.

The pumpkins roll, they're far from shy,
"Pick me, pick me!" they sing, oh my!
Squash in their coats of golden hue,
Wobble so proudly, just to amuse you.

Apples in baskets beg for a bite,
Whispers of cider, our hearts take flight.
With each pluck, a giggle echoes deep,
As nature's booth serves laughter to keep.

So in this season, let joy be rife,
With silly fruits bringing vibrant life.
For autumn's embrace is a comical race,
In fields of laughter, we find our place.

## Dancing with Abundance

In fields of ruby, the berries sway,
With every gust, they giggle and play.
Grapes join round, a merry band,
In grapevine twirls, take a stand!

The veggies march with a bouncy beat,
Turnips stumble on their leafy feet.
"Can you catch us? We giggle and roll!"
As laughter sprouts, filling the whole bowl.

Cherries crown the merry parade,
With fruit hats, oh what a charade!
Onions peek out, with their tearful grins,
Offering humor where laughter begins.

So come, let's dance in this vibrant throng,
With plumpness and joy where we all belong.
In the harvest air, oh let's make a toast,
To nature's bounty – our funny host!

## A Harvesting Heart

With baskets wide, we stroll through the rows,
Plucking the laughter that nature bestows.
Each apple winks, "We're ripe for the show!"
As we giggle and dance, feeling quite the glow.

The corn is towering, with stalks so high,
They whisper secrets, oh my, oh my!
Under the rows, the beets play hide-and-seek,
While pumpkins roll in, a little antique.

"Take me home!" each veggie shouts loud,
In this colorful harvest, we're joyously proud.
Tomatoes blush red, with humor to share,
While zucchini slips by, without a care!

As twilight descends, the laughter still plays,
In baskets of bounty, we'd surely stay.
For in every harvest, our hearts intertwine,
With laughter and love, oh isn't it divine?

## **Honeyed Memories**

In a place where the bees like to hum,
The fruits laugh loud, 'Oh, here we come!'
A pear in a hat, a peach with a tie,
They argue about who gets the next pie.

The apples play tag, they're speedy and sly,
While grapes start a band, oh my, oh my!
With drums made of leaves and a flute from a vine,
They sing of the sun, and everything's fine.

A fig jokes with zest, says, 'I'm quite a catch,'
While berries debate if they're sweet or a match.
But the laughter rings on, like a song from the past,
In this garden of giggles, the fun's built to last.

So let's toast to the cheer, the joy and the thrill,
In this fruity parade, there's always more still!
With honey dripped smiles and a rumble of mirth,
We celebrate giggles; oh, what a sweet earth!

## Beneath the Hanging Branches

Underneath the branches, the shadows play,
Where fruits spin tales of a sunny day.
An apple tells secrets to a shy kiwi,
While cherries burst out, oh, wouldn't you see?

A pear wears a wig, quite the sight I must say,
And how he groans, 'This is not my way!'
The plums roll their eyes, 'Not another charade!'
But laughter is ripe in this leafy parade.

The oranges conspire, with zest in their eyes,
To prank the bananas, oh what a surprise!
They slip on a peel and tumble with glee,
As everyone chuckles, a fine jubilee!

So come join the fun, shed your solemn face,
In this circus of flavors, there's always a place.
Underneath the leafy cover and best,
Let's laugh with the fruits, get lost in this fest!

## The Dance of Ripened Fruits

In the cool of the night, the fruits take the floor,
With mangoes that twirl and pears who adore.
They dance with the breeze, in rhythm so fine,
While the stars spout giggles, sharing the shine.

The berries bounce high, on tiny green shoes,
While lemons yell loud, 'Don't forget the blues!'
With every sweet pirouette, laughter ensues,
A jig of the juicy, no one can refuse.

The grapes spin around, a tight-knit bouquet,
As melons spin tales in their whimsical way.
The dance floor's a rainbow, a vibrant delight,
As peaches all ponder, 'Who's leading tonight?'

So lift up your spirits, and join every cheer,
With fruits in a frenzy, happiness near.
In this merry parade of juicy pursuits,
The laughter's contagious, come join in the hoots!

## Scent of Wilderness

In the wild where the fruits have a blast,
They mingle with freeness, oh, such joy amassed!
The berries wear crowns of curious dew,
While the apples declare, 'We're the best of the crew!'

A wild raspberry giggles, 'I'm tart and I'm bold!'
Though a cucumber grunts, 'I'm the one to be sold!'
The figs share a toast, with honey in sight,
While avocados just smirk, 'Oh, isn't this nice?'

The pumpkins stand proud, with their youthful grin,
While the nuts tell old tales of their heroic win.
Each fruit has a story, a whimsy to share,
In the wilderness wild, they're the life of the fair.

So take in the scents, so fruity and sweet,
In this land of wild laughter, they happily meet.
With chuckles and cheer, and a harvest to boast,
Let's celebrate nature; it's what we love most!

## **Colors Beyond the Horizon**

In the garden of giggles, fruits make a pact,
Apples wear smiles, and pears dance — intact.
Lemons throw parties, they're sweet with their zest,
While cherries play hide-and-seek, they're the best.

Pumpkins dress up with hats made of green,
While strawberries flirt like they're always seen.
Bananas slip out with their peels at the ball,
And grapes tumble down, they're the life of it all.

Cantaloupes chuckle beneath leafy shrouds,
As watermelons boast, tuning up their loud crowds.
Pineapples gossip in crowns, oh so proud,
Each fruit has a fun story, shared with the crowd.

So, if you visit, come quick with a grin,
The colors are laughing, let the fun begin!
Every slice holds a secret, each bite brings a cheer,
In this fruity court, there's nothing to fear.

## **Harvest Moon Serenade**

Under the moonlight, the veggies rehearse,
With pumpkins crooning, it's quite the verse.
Potatoes with tap shoes, they dance on the ground,
While broccoli bugs play their tunes all around.

Carrots in tuxedos, they sway with delight,
Kale whispers secrets well into the night.
Zucchini gets jealous, pulls faces with glee,
As tomatoes blush bright at the sight of the pea.

The chorus of corn sings as crickets applaud,
While beans take their bows, a little bit flawed.
On the harvest moon stage, it's quite the affair,
With laughter and snacks spreading joy through the air.

So join in the jesting, don't let it pass,
For under the moon, it's a veggie carnival, alas!
They'll serenade you 'til the first light of day,
In this whimsical garden, where laughter holds sway.

## Nestled Treasures of September

In September, the crunch brings treasures untold,
As apples embrace in their jackets of gold.
Nuts scatter laughter from tree boughs so high,
While bees throw a party — they buzz with a sigh.

Pumpkins are plotting a prank on the crows,
Who think they can peek at the harvest we chose.
Grapes spill their secrets, their wine whisper sweet,
As leaves twirl and wiggle, all dance to the beat.

Tomatoes blushing, donning hues of delight,
While peppers do pirouettes — what a sight!
Herbs in a circle, playing tic-tac-toe,
All bundled together in a jolly tableau.

So come join the romp in this patch of pure fun,
Where treasures are nestled like tricks in the sun.
September's a month where the laughter won't end,
With gardens of giggles, there's joy to expend.

## Juicy Conversations in the Breeze

The fruits have convened for a chat in the sun,
Strawberries share tales of their sweet little run.
Bananas boast loudly of slipping last year,
While oranges juggle — quite the talent, I fear.

Peaches roll in, with gossip that sings,
About lemons and limes, and their zesty bling.
Watermelons chuckle, dropping seeds in the air,
While cherries debate who's the best of the pair.

With every soft breeze, they giggle and tease,
Fruits laughing together, with so much to seize.
The juicy confessions spill out like fine wine,
In this quirky garden, where all things align.

So if you need laughter, just pop on by,
Join fruits in their chatter 'neath the wide-open sky.
In conversations so juicy, the fun won't cease,
With every sweet moment, it's a feast of peace!

## Fragrant Promises

The apples giggle, round and red,
As squirrels plot from their overhead.
"I'll have a snack!" one nutter calls,
While bumbling bees make careless falls.

The pears dance chaotically, oh what a sight,
With nectarines twirling in delight.
They toss ripe plums like confetti fair,
While cherries chuckle, spreading cheer everywhere.

Beneath the boughs, a raucous cheer,
As fruit and critters held so dear.
The wind whispers secrets with a grin,
As all the flavors tumble in.

## The Language of Petals

Petals chat softly in the breeze,
"I saw a bumblebee—did you see?"
They gossip about the sun's hot flair,
And flower's antics, with glad to share.

Roses wink and toss their heads,
Joking with daisies on their beds.
"Did you hear? The violets said,
'We're the fanciest ones,' they proudly tread.

Tulips play hide and seek with the sun,
While daffodils giggle, oh what fun!
All blooming with laughter, quite spry,
In this floral fiesta, oh my!

What a colorful riot of chatter and glee,
As petals delight in their jubilee.
Every bud has a jest, it's plain to see,
In this garden where humor is key.

## Quiet Surrender of Leaves

Leaves let go with a fluttering cheer,
As they tumble down without fear.
"I'm free!" one shouts, spinning about,
"Catch me if you can!" in a fizzy shout.

Crimson and gold twist in the air,
A leafy conga, without a care.
They chuckle and swirl, this autumn game,
In the crisp cool winds, they're never the same.

Rustling giggles ride on the breeze,
A symphony played by squirrels with ease.
"Look at us dancing!" they all exclaim,
In their crisp coats, like it's all a game.

Leaves laughing hard as they reach the ground,
Creating a blanket of joy all around.
Nature's own confetti, it swirls and bounds,
In this fun-filled fiesta, where joy resounds.

## The Tasting Hour

Plump berries, like jewels on display,
Tempt passersby who shout, "Hooray!"
"Is that raspberry tart?" someone inquires,
As fruit stands reveal their sugary pyres.

The peaches blush, all fuzzy and sweet,
As kids make faces, filling up with treats.
"I'll have a bite!" giggles a sprite,
In this tasting hour, all seems right.

Grapes tumble down in a juicy lane,
With sticky fingers and laughter that reigns.
"Spit the seeds!" someone yells with delight,
As watermelon juice brings such joy to the bite.

Cherry pits fly like a game of dodge,
While pie enthusiasts begin to plod.
In the whirlwind of flavors, no one stays sour,
It's all in good fun during this tasting hour.

## Cherries on the Wind

Cherries splat on the ground, oh what a sight,
A bird dives in, thinks it's quite a delight.
The squirrel nearby wears a crown made of red,
Chewing like royalty, quite proud of his bread.

Laughter erupts as they tumble and roll,
Chasing those berries, oh what a stroll!
Pit spitting contests, who can launch the best?
With each tiny victory, they laugh and they jest.

The raccoon joins in with a dance that's so slick,
Twirls 'round the branches, it's quite the trick!
Dewy-faced giggles echo through the trees,
As cherries on the wind make everyone sneeze!

So let's raise a glass to this berry parade,
With fruit hats and chuckles, we're never dismayed.
For laughter and chaos are always the rules,
In this wild fruity kingdom where we are the fools.

## The Language of Falling Leaves

Leaves tumble down like a merry parade,
Each one that flutters got secrets displayed.
The maple, the oak, and the birch all conspire,
To share tales of autumn, around fires they tire.

A whisper of wind tells a joke of the day,
Two leaves get tangled, they giggle and sway.
The acorns roll by with a raucous delight,
Squirrel stands guard, with plans for a bite.

Crisp crunches beneath as we waddle and leap,
Dodging those leaves that pile up in a heap.
A prank from the wind sends a shower of gold,
While laughter ignites in the air, uncontrolled.

In this wacky ballet of nature's surprise,
We join in the fun, let our spirits all rise.
The language of leaves, so silly and sweet,
Turns moments to memories, with nature's heartbeat.

## **Sweet Revolution Under Striped Skies**

Under striped skies, the fruit's having fun,
Peaches grow silly, like they're on the run.
Bananas unite for a grandier cause,
While grapefruits giggle, it's a fruit-filled applause.

Tomatoes take charge, shouting orders with zest,
"Let's overthrow salads, we'll put them to rest!"
With a battle of flavors, they jostle and shout,
A revolution of sweetness, no chance of a drought.

The cucumbers wobble, with humor unbound,
As they rally around, a salad-less ground.
While carrots debate their long-lasting plight,
"It's better to dance in the sun, full of light!"

Beneath the bold stripes, the laughter unfolds,
This riot of fruit, a story retold.
In each zany giggle, every burst of cheer,
The revolution blossoms, with joy ever near.

## **Boughs Heavy with Quiet Dreams**

Boughs droop low, with secrets to share,
Dreams interwoven, without a care.
A pear feels weighty with thoughts of the night,
While apples are giggling, feeling just right.

The plums start a contest, "Who can snore loud?"
Each thud of a fall draws a curious crowd.
Cherries conspire in whispers so sweet,
As bees buzz around, dancing on tiny feet.

The nightingale chuckles serenely above,
Sings lullabies sweetly, a tune full of love.
But the peaches just snicker, in fuzziness wrapped,
They'd rather tell jokes than dreams they've been clasped.

So let dreams hang heavy, but with laughter so light,
Underneath this old bough, we'll giggle till night.
Quiet dreams can frolic, in joyful surprise,
As fruit can be funny beneath starlit skies.

www.ingramcontent.com/pod-product-compliance
Lightning Source LLC
Chambersburg PA
CBHW060129230426
43661CB00003B/366